THE BLACK COLLAR MINDSET

THE BLACK COLLAR MINDSET

The Art of Strategic Thinking

SETH MILLER

First Printing, 2019

ISBN 978-0-578-49146-2

Paradigm Shift Consulting
2748 Autumn Harvest Lane
Belleville, IL 62221

DISCLAIMER
This book is for educational use only. The views in the book are of the author alone. The reader is responsible for his or her own actions. Adherence to all applicable laws and regulations, including international, federal, state, and local governing professional licensing, business practices, advertising and all other aspects of doing business in the United States, Canada, or any other jurisdiction is a sole responsibility of the purchaser or reader. The author assumes no responsibility or liability whatsoever on the behalf of the purchaser or reader if these material.

MAMA,

It's because of you, Monique and I have a "Must do" attitude. Thank you for being the ultimate hustler in our lives!JUNE 9 1960–∞

If

If you can keep your head when all about you
Are losing theirs and blaming it on you,
If you can trust yourself when all men doubt you,
But make allowance for their doubting too;
If you can wait and not be tired by waiting,
Or being lied about, don't deal in lies,
Or being hated, don't give way to hating,
And yet don't look too good, nor talk too wise:

If you can dream—and not make dreams your master;
If you can think—and not make thoughts your aim;
If you can meet with Triumph and Disaster
And treat those two impostors just the same;
If you can bear to hear the truth you've spoken
Twisted by knaves to make a trap for fools,
Or watch the things you gave your life to, broken,
And stoop and build 'em up with worn-out tools:

If you can make one heap of all your winnings
And risk it on one turn of pitch-and-toss,
And lose, and start again at your beginnings
And never breathe a word about your loss;
If you can force your heart and nerve and sinew
To serve your turn long after they are gone,
And so hold on when there is nothing in you
Except the Will which says to them: 'Hold on!'

If you can talk with crowds and keep your virtue,
Or walk with Kings—nor lose the common touch,
If neither foes nor loving friends can hurt you,
If all men count with you, but none too much;
If you can fill the unforgiving minute
With sixty seconds' worth of distance run,
Yours is the Earth and everything that's in it,
And—which is more—you'll be a Man, my son!

By Rudyard Kipling

To my Kellon,

There are so many things that I wish we could have shared: long talks about life, your thoughts about God, and who you are versus who people want you to be. Son, you will experience things you won't be able to understand at the time, and I may not be there to help you along the way. This book is for you and others looking for "the answers." Life has a way of connecting with you; you just have to listen. These forms of meaningful communication may be through family members, schoolmates, even people you aren't that fond of. Remember, you have a purpose in life, and it takes time to understand it. Some people leave this world without tapping into their potential. I hope this book will give you an idea of how I found ways to discover who I am and who you are meant to be, which is Great!

Love, Dad

TABLE OF CONTENTS

MENTOR TO MENTEE
BY VANJEWEL

WHEN I THINK of Seth the Speaker, I am reminded of another phenomenon that I witnessed.

Throughout my life, I have planted many gardens that have produced a variety of fruits and vegetables.

Any experienced gardener can attest that merely planting seeds does not guarantee a fruitful crop. The soil must be nourished, the plants must be tended, and nature must cooperate in their growth and maturity. Seeds must be planted under the right conditions or they will not germinate.

A few years ago, I planted a row of mustard green seeds which yielded modest crop of mustard greens.

As the month passed and the leaves on the plant withered in the summer's intense heat, I began to concentrate my efforts on other plants in the garden that thrived in such conditions.

After a long hot summer, autumn offered another opportunity to plant more mustard greens; however, my schedule would not allow me to devote much time to a fall crop, so I decided against planting a garden at all.

One winter day, I glanced outside my window at my garden. I saw what appeared to be a plant that was approximately four inches tall. Certainly, that is not a mustard green plant growing in the dead of winter, or so I thought. As a approached the garden, I could see that this was indeed a mustard green plant. Over several weeks, the plant produced a magnitude of leaves which I picked and cooked. This one plant produced more food than all of the other plants combined.

After a few weeks, I noticed a flower growing from within the plant. The flower eventually produced seeds that I harvested to use for future crops. The life of a single plant continues to provide nourishment for me and my family, as does Seth.

Seth is a vibrant plant in my life. He has been the plant that has yielded so many positive results throughout many seasons.

While, I have always had faith that he would do well in life, I have been truly amazed at how he has flourished over the years.

When I met Seth, I was impressed with the wealth of knowledge and wisdom he possessed at such a young age. The things he said to me made perfect sense, so I applied several of those things to my personal and professional life. As a result, I have reaped countless benefits from his advice and his friendship. His ability to listen, learn and teach have been very instrumental in the lives of countless people from all walks of life.

Our professional lives have placed a physical distance between us, but I still count on him for inspiration and guidance in all my important decisions. He has remained constant in helping me to achieve my goals.

Like my lone mustard green plant, Seth produces positive results under conditions that appear to be abnormal. He provides essential nutrients for a healthy and successful life. He brings the joy of things expected. Given the opportunity, he will provide you with food for the soul and leave you with seeds to plant your next crop.

I am pleased to introduce this young man to those who have not had the privilege and pleasure to meet him. Ladies and gentlemen...Seth, and the *Black Collar Mindset*.

FOREWORD BY
ADRIAN GARRISON
AND
CORRIS JACKSON

I MET AN ANGEL in a foxhole in Afghanistan. Not only in a physical form, but in a mental one, too, because mentally, I was at war with myself. I could have easily taken the road most traveled and used every excuse in the proverbial book to justify my internal pain. But...my spiritual higher being brought Seth into my life! He was an angel. Not the stereotypical white-robed, halo-wearing, floating kind, but the keep-it-real, exactly-what-I-needed, right-on-time kind of angel.

As you dig deeper into the pages of this book, you too can have that "angel in the foxhole." No matter if you are a man or a woman, black or white or other, the words in this book will reach down into your core and open your mentality to greater heights. This book will awaken that thing...the thing that's deep down in your soul, the thing that has been yearning to explode out of your body to show the world (and yourself) how great you are. In this book, Seth gives you the raw, in-your-face, no-excuses reality that all of us need to awaken the hustle we all have within. This book isn't a collection of sappy social memes, it is a guide to understanding how to think strategically so that you can achieve your greatest potential. What are you waiting for? Start reading, challenge yourself, motivate yourself, and become the best you can be.

ADRIAN GARRISON

Have you ever seen athletes who are considered five-star recruits? Normally, their reputations speak for themselves. Now, let's imagine that you actually got to witness firsthand the incredible talent the person possesses. There's no doubt you would be a believer, but to have the honor of befriending and mentoring that individual seems to be the greater blessing. Well, the aforementioned scenario is how I became friends with Seth (aka Seth The Speaker, aka DJ Scooby, aka Air Force SNCO MSgt Miller, aka My Great Friend). From the first time I talked with Seth, I knew this dude was cut from a different cloth. I quickly noticed he was an old soul with the ability to meet any person anywhere they're at—he can just as easily connect with a homeless person, a person of high esteem, a regular Joe on the street, or a high roller on Wall Street. He is someone I love talking with because he listens and always gets it. Additionally, he is always sincerely appreciative of any nuggets of knowledge you bestow upon him. Seth is also wise enough to provide even those who are his seniors with great advice. Many times during our conversations, he seems to become the mentor, and I have so much respect for him that I gladly accept what he is telling me without any reservations. Like the five-star recruit, Seth's reputation speaks for itself, and when you read his body of work, it's like watching a soaring film—you will quickly buy into this rising star and take action! Most importantly, as we have become great friends over time and our wives have connected with each other, I have seen firsthand just how great this guy is. I've become part of his inner circle and extended family just as he has become part of mine. I hold this guy in high esteem, and I would literally give him the shirt off my back because I know that in turn, he would quickly put a Black Collar Clothing T-shirt or sweater on mine. Seth, you are a great man, father, servant, and hustler, but most of all, you're a great friend. I thank God for meeting you and becoming your friend...and your Brother. Whoever reads this book will gain intangible keys to success! So right on, bro, right on. Keep hustling, hitting the gym, and getting your full sexy on!

CORRIS JACKSON

WHAT IS THE
BLACK COLLAR
MINDSET?

BEFORE ANSWERING THAT question, I would like to ask you one first. Have you ever heard the term "blue-collar worker"? A blue-collar worker is a working-class person who performs manual labor, like a skilled manufacturing worker, a factory operator, a sanitation worker, or a technician. These jobs typically involve more physical skills than they do administrative work. The reference to a "blue collar" comes from the traditional industrial uniform, which is typically a heavyweight blue-collared shirt.

Now, let's talk about the "white-collar worker." This is someone who may perform office or administrative work. Consider them to be "non-manual workers." Their duties may include but are not limited to administrative work, book-keeping, or computer programming/usage. The reference to a "white collar" comes from the typical white dress shirt or blouse worn with a business suit while working in an office setting.

Finally, there's the "black-collar worker." To many people, that means someone who's involved in some sort of criminal activity—a person of the underworld, or even a villain, for goodness' sake. That's a myth. The truth is that black-collar workers are passionate artists, singers, clothing designers, music producers, even beauticians who work for themselves after working for others.

You may be reading this and be employed by an industry that requires you to wear a blue or white collar, but I feel you have more to offer. In order to do things that may be uncommon for others, you have to think uncommonly. This book will provide you with ways to maneuver skillfully around individuals who think in conventional, noncreative ways. Within these pages are gems that—if applied—could change your life, gems that could help the people you hold dear to your heart.

DISCLAIMER: This is not a "you're going to feel all mushy and gushy inside" type of book. This book is meant to challenge you to be accountable for your current situation and to take meaningful actions from this day forward. The words you'll read may not be politically correct or even nice. Neither is the world, so get over it. I'm probably not someone you'd want to listen to or hang out with unless you are ready to evolve and elevate, because I won't sit there and let you complain about life and wear your pain like it's something to be proud of. Now, get something to write with. This is [insert your name here] _____'s book. You'll only get out of this what you put into this. Let's go!

YOU ARE A
FORCE

"Don't underestimate the Force."

—DARTH VADER

"I was always looking outside myself for strength and confidence, but it comes from within. It is there all the time."

—ANNA FREUD

Gotta love the 80s! It was a time of great music and questionable attire worn by everyone. One thing about the 80s I enjoyed most of all was the movies, those majestic, action-packed science-fiction cult-classic blobs of goodness! Not only is Vader's line the best introduction possible to this section, there will be many other references to the 80s, partially because they're easy to relate to and partially because now, at the ripe age of 37, I understand how powerful 80s movies in particular were. Plus, now younger readers have a reason to go to the video store and rent a few of these jewels. Wait a minute, I almost lost you... Netflix! Go to Netflix!

I wrote this book as an easy-to-read tool you can use to unleash *your* potential Force within. Even though I'm not a Star Wars buff, it doesn't take long for anyone to understand what the Force is in Star Wars and what it references in real life: the Force is a metaphysical and ubiquitous power in the Star Wars fictional universe, and likewise, you have this "thing" inside of you that is so powerful that at times it may frighten you. Let's call that the Force, too.

When you apply laser focus to a goal, deadline, or dream, the results can be astronomical. The key is to understand that this focus, this Force, comes from within you. Outside influences also contribute to your Force: your family members, social groups, and perhaps a church. Ultimately, though, the decision on whether or not to press forward is *your* decision.

The Force is a symbol of your consciousness. To get even more profound, the Force helps you awaken your consciousness by acknowledging and vindicating the inner you and by recognizing and limiting your ego. Your personal Force is so powerful that it can spark a flame in someone else's life, too. Everything you say and do has some effect on the people around you, be it positive or negative. Even total strangers are impacted. Think about it—when you snap at a salesclerk or lay on the horn because the guy in front of you stopped at a green light, just as you've affected them, they will impact others, who will impact others...and the downward spiral will continue.

But the positivity of your inner Force is waiting for you! Your gifts and talents are lying dormant, waiting for you to permit them to manifest. If you knew about the potential locked inside of you and crying out to be released, would you let it out? Many people die without ever releasing it—they take their potential with them when they leave this world. Maybe you have big goals, or maybe you have small goals that won't overly test your limits. Either way, you will never know the extent of what you can become if you don't get out of your comfort zone.

By the way, hush the negative chatter! Many times, it comes from someone you care about or trust. They may not realize that the information they're giving you could deter you from pursuing your dreams. A lot of the time, when someone is giving you advice, they are trying to protect you from winding up with financial issues or wasting your time. Too often, they say something negative instead of saying, "But you can do it!" or "Try this instead." Beware of people who want to give you advice about something they have never personally done before. Your dreams might be too much for them to comprehend. Good! That information wasn't theirs in the first place. Once you come to understand and know who is truly in your circle, keep it small and close. Your circle can and should consist of people who have the same passions and dreams as you do.

Your circle might include a mentor who keeps you in line and on track. Sometimes we get to the point of only hearing our ideas, and to us, they are the best ideas in the world. But even though the results could be excellent, we may not know how to achieve them. Utilize your circle to vet your ideas and shape your Force. The right kind of circle will tell you what they hear and will hold you accountable. In a perfect world, your circle would consist of family members and maybe childhood friends, but that's not always realistic. As your goals expand, your perspectives about life will expand as well, so do not be surprised if your family members or spouse aren't able to help cultivate your Force. You may have to look outside of your everyday associates to find like-minded people to include in your circle.

We tend to gravitate to what *feels* good, not what necessarily *is* good for us. Still, sometimes we find ourselves in uncomfortable situations that create nervousness or worry. That's when it's wise to convert stress to "eustress." Eustress is a good form of stress that can increase your performance, your happiness, and your sense of well-being. Although eustress is a type of stress, it need not be damaging to your body. Unlike chronic stress (which *is* taxing on your body), eustress does not have any unfavorable effects—instead, it lifts your spirits and helps you stay in a good mood. Eustress provides the desired balance by balancing out the negative stress.

Why don't you see what you are made of? Fear is a driver for most if not all of the decisions we make every day: "Will I fail? Will I succeed and keep it up? Will I get hurt? Will I hurt someone?" Your fears are based on your immediate perceptions of false emotions appearing real or you having the urge to forget everything and run. You have to push past those fears and knee-jerk impulses, because the limits you (often unconsciously) impose on yourself can shape your view of life and everything and everyone around you.

We wake up every day blessed to have another opportunity to show the world what we've got, and the Force wakes up with us! Understanding the strength of the Force inside of you is just one step towards being a better you.

THE WRAP-UP

TRUST THAT VOICE inside of you! It will challenge you to be what you know you can be. Don't run from it or try to drown it out with distractions. That voice will activate the Force within you that's pushing you to be magnificent! I promise you this: when you allow the Force to move you, it will defy and redefine what you thought was normal. Get ready for the ride of your life! The best YOU is within reach.

ACCOUNTABILITY SHEET

My Force Is:

Write down all of the gifts that are inside of you.

_____

_____

_____

What talents do you have that people thank you for? For example, are you helpful, are you a lover of learning, or do you encourage others?

_____

_____

_____

IN THE NEXT 24 HRS, I WILL...

_____

_____

_____

_____

_____

_____

_____

_____

_____

_____

_____

_____

_____

_____

_____

_____

_____

_____

_____

_____

_____

_____

_____

_____

_____

_____

THOUGHT

*"We are what our thoughts have made us, so take
care about what you think. Words are secondary.
Thoughts live; they travel far."*

—SWAMI VIVEKANANDA

I REMEMBER PLAYING childhood games in elementary
school, games like foursquare and basketball. One game I
got pretty good at was checkers. No one could beat me at
checkers! If you aren't familiar with the game, each player
begins the game with 12 colored discs. Typically, one set of
pieces is black and the other is red. Each player places his or
her checkers on the 12 dark squares closest to him or her. The
player with the black checkers moves first, and then the play-
ers alternate moves. The checkerboard consists of 64 squares,
alternating between 32 dark and 32 light squares. The checkers are positioned so that each player has a light square on the
right-hand corner that's closest to him or her. A player wins
the game when their opponent cannot make a move. In most
cases, that happens when all of the opponent's pieces are gone
or blocked. When I played, sometimes would I anticipate my
opponent's moves because I knew the possible steps and
could map the moves out in my head.

Much like the ability to win at checkers depends on being able to predict the sequence of moves, the fastest way to prevent hurting other people is to think about the ramifications your words will have. More people are beaten down by words than fists. Do you really need to say something hurtful? How would you feel if someone were to say that to you or about you? Are you using being honest as an excuse to say something harmful? When you're hurting yourself, does it help to lash out with your own hurtful words? Many of the wisest and most considerate people in the world are thought to be wise and considerate because they *don't* speak impulsively—they allow themselves time to consider their words before they say them.

An acronym that's helped me have better conversations is W.A.I.T. It stands for "Why Am I Talking?" Not only is it best to pause before speaking, it's also wise to ask yourself "Is what I want to say necessary?" Sometimes we fall short when it comes to this because of long-time habits, one of which is that of course we love to hear the sound our voice! We're *us*!

That said, your voice isn't always needed. Take the time to sit back and listen more and speak less. Your mouth can get you into a world of trouble if you speak just from your emotions. Some things need to be said, yes, but everything should be considered prior to being spoken. Before you speak, ask yourself, "What's at risk if what I say doesn't come out right?" If there's a possibility that your words could damage a relationship or hurt someone's feelings, don't say them. If you say, "Don't take this the wrong way, but..." chances are that someone *will* take your words the wrong way. It's best to just not preface your words that way. Is it so hard to find other ways to say what you need to say? If you matter to that person, they will hear you. Think from a place of love and communicate from that same place. You'll be good to go!

THE WRAP-UP

WE ALL CAN take the time to think about things before we do or say them. The definition of a mistake is an action or judgment that is misguided or wrong, and it's easier to make a mistake if you don't take the time to consider your words and actions. Thus, I encourage you to consider a few things before you say something. First, what's more important: the conversation or the person? Make sure you actively listen to *all* of what someone else is saying before you say something that could damage the relationship. Second, check your emotions at the door. We sometimes say things based on pure emotions that we regret saying later. Ask yourself, "Am I upset about this situation?" If the answer is yes, then W.A.I.T.! And third, remember W.A.I.T. ("Why Am I Talking?") and try to practice this technique. Taking your time and evaluating *why* you're about to say what you're about to say could save you many unnecessary headaches.

IT'S P.O.P.,
NOT SODA

"My mission in life is not merely to survive, but to thrive;
and to do so with some passion, some compassion, some humor, and some style."

—MAYA ANGELOU

"POP" VERSUS "SODA." For most of my life, I referred to Coke as "pop," Sprite as "pop," off-brand soft drinks as "pop." It wasn't until I went into the military outside of Detroit that I heard people refer to soft drinks as "soda." It threw me for a loop! I didn't understand it. I thought that soda is the carbonation that's added to the flavored syrup to make "pop." Who knows? My logic was probably backward then...probably still is. However, now the word "pop" has a different meaning for me.

This chapter is going to be all about the *acronym* P.O.P. It stands for Passion, Opportunity, and Purpose. We all have a passion; what we fail to do is listen to it or engage with it. Passion could be anything we love to do, or it could be what we think about throughout the day as we're working. Even while we're sleeping or doing mundane activities, we still have something at the back of our minds that we would love to do. Your passion could actually wake you up in the morning without an alarm clock! When you are pursuing your passion, time flies by and material things seem to not matter as much anymore.

Let's look at the Opportunity part of P.O.P. and think about the opportunities you have to utilize your passion. Say you love to cook—it's your passion. You could be preparing food not just for yourself, but for other people. That's an opportunity. Maybe you could cook for other people on a larger scale by opening a restaurant. Is there a building in your area you could purchase? Is there shared space where you could start a pop-up restaurant to see how your culinary vision could flourish? Is there a trade school nearby that teaches culinary arts? Maybe you could learn or work there. No matter which avenue you choose, surrounding yourself with you passionate people is always a plus.

Possibilities are endless if you just look for them. I once read, "Many opportunities are born out of failures." Failures represent a hub for opportunities—all you need to do to find them is focus on them. Think about Thomas Edison, the creator of the light bulb. He tried making his idea reality over a thousand times before it worked. When he was asked why he didn't give up, he responded, "It took me one thousand steps to get it right." He turned his failures into opportunities. Remember, there is an opportunity in behind every closed door! Just knock. A single opportunity can become fruitful and rewarding.

The last part of P.O.P. is your Purpose. Your life's purpose consists of your motivations, aka the reasons you get out of bed in the morning. Your purpose can guide your life decisions, influence your behavior, determine your value-based goals, and give you a sense of direction. For some people, their purpose is what gives their lives meaning and satisfying work.

Everyone has a purpose in this life. It may not be evident to others; sometimes, it might not even be apparent to you. But don't run away from your purpose! Your purpose in life should be more significant than your current situation. How will your purpose affect others? How will you teach and lead others so they can also benefit from your purpose?

THE WRAP-UP

EVALUATING YOUR PASSION, Opportunities, and Purpose can be useful in any situation. Whenever you aren't sure about a new job or relationship, do a P.O.P. analysis. If you think this technique sounds a little bit selfish, good! It is, and there's nothing wrong with that. Consider your time and space to be extremely precious from now on. Starting now, anything you do or even think about doing should be worth your effort. Ask yourself, "Am I passionate about this? Do I see opportunities to grow? Am I walking in my purpose?" If you answer "no" to any of those questions, then why are you doing it?

Do not let others confuse you or pressure you about your purpose. For many reasons, sometimes people will try to pressure you into doing something that you really don't want to do. One of those reasons might be that they want to live vicariously through you—they might feel like they don't have enough youth, money, or ambition to do what they want to do, so now you "should" do it even if it doesn't suit your purpose. But nope! Don't. If something is not in line with you and your purpose, you can only fake it for so long. Trust me—do you!

ACCOUNTABILITY SHEET

What's Your P.O.P.?

What do you love? What is your PASSION?

_____

_____

_____

How could you exercise your passion? What are your
OPPORTUNITIES?

_____

_____

_____

What does the world need? What is your PURPOSE?

_____

_____

_____

IN THE NEXT 24 HRS, I WILL...

EVERYONE CAN'T
COME WITH YOU

"Not everyone who starts with you will finish with you. Be willing to go without them if you have to."

—TONY GASKINS

LET'S FACE IT—WHEN you have a dream and a goal that is yours, it's yours and only yours. It's great if individuals can see your dreams and goals, and it's even better if they can come along for the ride. However, that's not reality, at least not all of the time. Individuals are not meant to go with you on your whole journey through life. You may already know what some of your ventures are going to be and you may have crystal-clear vision as to what your end goals are, yet other people may not see or understand where you're headed. That's okay. They don't need to understand your vision to be able to gravitate towards you and help you get to where you need to be. Keep that in mind when you want to go to the next level. The individuals who were there for you in the beginning may not be the same individuals who are there at the end, and that's okay as well. That's not an easy pill to swallow, I know...but it's reality.

I've had dreams and aspirations of doing amazing things in this life, and sometimes, I actually attempt them. One year, for example, I wanted to put on an event to help bring awareness to veterans dealing with PTSD and suicide. In my head, it was going to be a great event: I could picture every Armed Forces member in uniform alongside their spouses and dependents, and everyone would be celebrating this event for a much-needed cause. I took a leap of faith and communicated my idea to a group of individuals whom I thought would believe in the vision and understand the goal.

In the beginning, about 15 to 20 of the people I talked to agreed that my idea was great and said they would be on board. I explained that I couldn't do everything myself—that would have been a disaster—and that when a task needed to be accomplished that I wasn't skilled to do, I would ask one of the people who supported my idea to help out. I made sure people knew that my vision would require people to volunteer their time, meaning zero payment. I had to manage the various tasks that would be needed and take care of the expenses, i.e., the overall costs, the venue costs, the keynote speaker fee, etc. I realized that I had to surround myself with individuals who wanted to get things done just as much as I did.

As the date of the event neared, I realized something else: the people who were there in the beginning were not truly invested in the vision the way they had they said they were. Remember those 15 to 20 people I started with? There were actually 7 solid people at the end of the day.

Nevertheless, the result was an awesome event! Over 100 participants of all ranks of Armed Forces members attended, and through this meaningful event, we were able to raise money for a nonprofit organization called Mission 22. The night of the event was the night I realized that not everybody is meant to come with you all the way. With that in mind, we still have to choose our teams correctly. (More about that in later chapters.) If you start to change your vision or do something different, people may react in different ways—some may be happy for you, some may be indifferent, some may be puzzled, some may respond in negative or discouraging ways. Many of these reactions are probably not so much about you but about the person who had those reactions and the state of his/her life. How they feel about themselves comes through in the words they use and the judgments they make. So, remember: when there's somewhere you want to go, your passenger seat may be empty, and that's okay.

THE WRAP-UP

THE WHOLE VETERAN'S Day experience taught me that not everybody is meant to come along for the ride. I'm sure you have been in a similar situation. It's not a good feeling when somebody in your crew says one thing to your face but their actions show something else. Trust me, I know that feeling very well. The trick is to stay focused on your goal and watch how they move. Don't spend too much time wondering why people aren't jumping on board with your idea! Maybe they have something going on that is more important and it's just none of your business. Other people may not know how to say, "Sorry—I want to help, but I don't know how to do what you need me to do."

In the future, if you have a wild idea and you want a friend's buy-in, explain what you are thinking and ask your friend how they can help you be successful. On the other hand, sometimes people don't want to be associated with the possibility that your idea may not succeed, and you know what? It might not! That's a common fear we all may encounter at some point. The good part is that you can still learn how to work together as a team and how to trust each other on different levels. It's better to fail and learn as a team than to succeed and celebrate alone.

YOU HEAR

"Realize now the power that your words command if you simply choose them wisely."

—TONY ROBBINS

B E CAREFUL OF the things you hear from people, especially when they're talking about other people. You may be talking to a hater! I remember a time when a good friend of mine told me a secondhand story about someone. What my friend didn't know was that I knew the other person very well, and I knew the other side of the story. After listening to my friend talk about a guy he didn't know, I asked him a couple of questions: "Were you there? Do you know if that story is true? Why do you think it's true? Do you have all of the evidence?" Based on his answers, he realized that he had fallen into a preconceived trap.

Sometimes we let what people tell us stop us from finding our truth. People close to you will tell you what to do or not to do based on their experiences and level of education. (Not in terms of formal education, necessarily, but also in terms of life lessons and common sense. One of the smartest and wisest men I've ever known had a third-grade education.) No one who truly cares for you wants to see you hurt in the same way they were, of course, even though you are a different person and your truth is yours to find.

The hard fact is that we often listen to others and heed their advice to quit before we even start to pursue our goals. If I had listened to my friends in Detroit, I would not have enlisted in the greatest Air Force in the world over twenty years ago, but I'm sure glad I did! Take time to research information for yourself. Often, we listen to people who have limited information on a subject just because we love them or respect them. They may even have experience related to the subject at hand, but you are a different person and your situation may be different. Always listen to what people say, but then *you* have to decide what and who works for you. Listen to people's intentions through their words and actions.

Others persevere in achieving their goals and encourage you to keep going, too, reminding you that whatever you want is possible. If someone tells you what you shouldn't do or tries to discourage you from achieving your goal, don't get defensive—instead, ask about their experiences. At that point, they'll either stop talking or give you useful information that will help you avoid pitfalls. Never underestimate the knowledge of others, because not everyone is a hater. Many people *do* want to see you win.

THE WRAP-UP

THE WORDS YOU digest become part of you if you subscribe to them. You've heard the statement "You are what you eat," right? You are also what you hear and consume. Every day, we have a choice of whether or not to listen to false truths about ourselves and our goals. Not everyone means you ill will—they might just be regurgitating what they themselves have heard or seen. Ask the important questions, like, "Were you there? Do you know if that story is true? Why do you think it's true? Do you have all of the evidence?" Don't let someone place their insecurities on you. It's bad juju!

ACCOUNTABILITY SHEET

Who do you tell your dreams to?

_____

_____

_____

How do they encourage/discourage you?

_____

_____

_____

What have you learned from the information you have
received from others?

_____

_____

_____

IN THE NEXT 24 HRS, I WILL...

MISTAKE

"A mistake that makes you humble is better than an achievement that makes you cocky."

—Anonymous

"When you make a mistake, there are only three things you should ever do about it: admit it, learn from it, and don't repeat it."

—Paul Bear Bryant

One thing that used to be difficult and hurtful to me was admitting to a mistake. That's because I take pride in my work, and perfection has always been a goal of mine. It wasn't until recently that I understood that making mistakes is part of the process of reaching perfection. I encourage you not to get "too big for your britches," to use an old-school term. You too are susceptible to slipping up from time to time. Why? Because you're human! Did you forget? It's not a matter of *if* you will mess up, it's a matter of *when*. The key is to get back up and then improve your circumstances so that you don't fall the same way again.

One more time for the people in the back: get back up and then improve your circumstances! Fail forward! Don't just quit—learn from what you've done and refine your approach. It's funny how life works. You may try to do something new that's outside of what your family and friends think you should do, and the whole time, you might be hearing that you shouldn't do it for whatever reason. You might fail the first time you try...or the second...or the third. But no matter how many times you attempt it and fail, get back up! People are still watching you. Some of them want to see when you will stop, if you'll stop, or why you won't. Nevertheless, they are watching, and they are silently inspired by your ambition. You have the power to change how people view you by staying focused on you and not them. Failure is healthy! Just try to improve yourself and your current situation along the way.

When you do fail, don't stay there face-down focusing on what didn't go right or who saw you fall. People who care about you are focused on how you will recover from your mishap. I've never met anyone who has made it in life without failing at something once, twice, three times. Put a plan into action to avoid the same pitfalls. Learn from every hill and dip you encounter in life—that way, every time you're standing on a peak, you'll be able to see how much you've learned.

We all want a better future, but we don't always have honest talks with ourselves about why we aren't where we want to be. For example, did you say that you wanted to lose 20 pounds last year? How did that work out for you? If you didn't meet your goal, chances are you never changed the bad habits you know you need to ditch to get the results you want. You have to think differently about how you've done things so that you can do them more effectively. Ask yourself what worked, what didn't, what should you improve, and what should you scrap. Writing down those items can help you dial into your goals and stay on the right path.

Another way to hold yourself accountable is to write a statement of intent to yourself. The exercise below will help remove excuses by helping you identify what or who has been in your way in the past. Vow to never let whatever or whoever that is get in your way again! Let's give it a try:

I will commit (_____ amount of time) to achieve
_____. I will avoid_____ and _____
in order to achieve_____. By (_____date), I
will have achieved _____.

Signed,_____.

By doing this exercise, you are writing down your goal twice, assigning a time frame and a date of completion for your goal, and signing your goal for self-accountability. Put this statement of intent someplace you'll see it every day so that you're reminded of it every day. This is *your* story. Be bold enough to get up and live your best life!

THE WRAP-UP

ONE OF THE worst things we can assume is that we are going to accomplish whatever we want whenever we want. That's crap! Who said you won't ever fail? I feel like if you fail and have the nerve to get up again, *that's* when you are winning. The loser stays down, looking crazy. You have everything in you to make it, but you have to get into the mindset that winning takes losing. Your strength comes from failure. It's like going to the gym: once you've pushed yourself to where you have to stop, make a note of that as your baseline so that the next time, you'll know your limits and push pass them. Hold yourself accountable. Give yourself room to fail, but don't allow room for excuses. If you give 100% towards your goals, I guarantee you won't be upset with your results.

ACCOUNTABILITY SHEET

Self-Accountability Statement
(fill out on a Monday or Sunday)

I will commit (_____ amount of time) to
achieve _____. I will avoid_____
and _____ in order to achieve_____.
By (_____date), I will have achieved
_____.

Signed,_____.

Bonus! Have your Accountability Partner sign, too:
_____.

Reflection Statement
(fill out on a Friday or Sunday)

I committed (_____ amount of time) to
achieve _____. I avoided_____
and _____ in order to achieve_____.
I'm (_____) closer to achieving
(_____).

I feel/felt (_____).

Signed,_____.

Bonus! Have your Accountability Partner sign, too:
_____.

IN THE NEXT 24 HRS, I WILL...

OR BENEFICIAL?

"Just because someone desires you does not mean that they value you."

—ANONYMOUS

WOULD YOU AGREE that we all have unique gifts? Some of us know how to tap into our gifts better than others do, but still, we all have them. When you walk with a certain level of pride in your step, people can see that there's something different about you, something that attracts people. You might have heard that kind of walk called "swagger." People love it! There will come a time when your inner Force will attract people to you, and when it does, you have to be mindful of *why* it does.

Years ago, back when I wanted to be a DJ, I thought being a DJ was just a matter of me playing music for people in exchange for payment. Wrong! DJing is a serious job that also happens to be fun. The skill comes from not only being able to play the right music at the right time, but being able to bring people onto the dance floor. And not just some people, all people! To me, music is universal the same way math is, and if music is used correctly, it can solve the problems of the world. (Is that wishful thinking? Lofty, I know. I have a soft spot for music and the people who love it.)

But back to my point. When I became a better DJ, more DJing gigs started coming my way. I eventually started wondering *why* I was getting so many gigs. Was I really that good? Yes and no! Due to being in the Air Force, I was able to travel around the world, and to keep me occupied when time was moving slowly, I would DJ. Some of my fellow Armed Forces members read books, took college classes, watched movies, or played video games, but music was what kept me distracted from what I was missing back home.

Maybe it was just a coincidence, but I always seemed to deploy over the Christmas holidays. However, I was always able to play holiday music for different squadrons, and when I did, for a moment I would think I was back home amongst friends and family, and in a sense, I was. We all were. Some people would tell me that for that one night, they would almost forget they were thousands of miles away from home. Over time, I became versatile enough to play any venue no matter the season or genre for hours on end, but I didn't know my worth. I would DJ an event for up to six hours and provide all of my own equipment for $150. Of course I would get business pouring in!

There's a difference between being a go-to person and being a sucker. Be a person of value, because your gifts and time are precious. Also, understand the difference between your value and your worth and know that not everyone will be able to see your worth. It's up to *you* to know your value and prove your worth.

"Worth" is a term used to denote how much something will cost. Your value, though, is a little deeper. What do you bring to the table? Are you the best at it? Can you be easily replaced? Ask yourself these kinds of questions to identify your worth *and* your value. Another way to figure out your worth and value is to ask a friend how much would they pay someone to do what you know how to do. Don't expect them to pay that price, of course—that's what a "homie hook-up" is for. (Side note: you can't stay in business if you're only giving "hook-ups," so dole them out sparingly.) Go online and research what the going rates are in your field or industry. How much are other people charging for the same service? While they may have been doing it for longer than you have, at least you can set a baseline. And remember that just because someone has been doing something for longer than you doesn't mean they are better at doing it than you are. Don't let less time spent in the game deter you. Follow your passion and seek out opportunities to use that passion for a larger purpose. Think "P.O.P."!

THE WRAP-UP

KNOW THE DIFFERENCE between quantity and quality. Ruminate about what you want to do and determine if it's in line with your value-based goals. Ask yourself, "Why do I want to do this? Is it only for the money or is it for the movement? Is it to impress or impact others?" Questions like these can keep you grounded and focused on the bigger picture, namely your "why."

ACCOUNTABILITY SHEET

What business are you in or want to be in?

_____

_____

_____

How much do you charge per hour or per project?

_____

_____

_____

How much are your competitors charging?

_____

_____

_____

Are you higher or lower? Why?

_____

_____

_____

IN THE NEXT 24 HRS, I WILL...

KEEP IT
MOVING

"Just smile and wave, boys!"

—KRESLEY COLE

"It's not the mountain ahead that wears you out; it's the grain of sand in your shoes."

—ROBERT W. SERVICE

I remember when my daughter Simonne, who was three years old at the time, taught me a valuable lesson: don't sweat the small stuff. We were at Walmart just picking up some things for the house. She was at the age where she would wave and smile at everyone like she was a little penguin. She would even try to give people high fives. Some people would acknowledge her, but others wouldn't pay attention to her. However, during this particular outing, someone blatantly ignored my baby!

Here's the scene: I was reaching for some sugar when I noticed a woman walking towards us. My daughter noticed her, too, and my baby girl smiled at the woman like she had been smiling at everybody during our entire Walmart safari. Then she put up her tiny hands for a high five. The lady looked at her and just rolled right past in her buggy. Can you imagine how upset I was? We're talking about my three-year-old daughter!

All kinds of levels of rage and anger came upon me. My thought at the moment was, "This is why we're at where we're at! Some people don't even have the common decency to wave at kids! How rude!" While I was contemplating high-fiving that rude lady in the face, my daughter was smiling and waving and high-fiving the next person she saw. She taught me not to sweat the small stuff and keep it moving. Likewise, I encourage you to keep going no matter what. Don't look for validation or "big ups" from people who don't care about what you're doing. They can't stop you!

I challenge you to think about the things you're doing right now. Are you doing those things from the right place? You'll realize one of two things: either you're not worrying about who's giving you accolades and recognition for the things you're doing, or you want social proof to show others how hot you are. But do not worry about getting validation for doing the things you're doing! If you are serving others, you're going to get the recognition you need. As I said, I was contemplating high-fiving that lady in the face, but my daughter showed me a better way. Take it from her and be a penguin—it looks fun!

THE WRAP-UP

THE MOTIVATIONAL SPEAKER Les Brown once said, "If you do things for you, it'll die with you, but if you do things for people, it will last forever." Our pride can sometimes get in the way of what's truly important, because along with our pride comes emotions that may not be accurate at the time. Remember to ask yourself, "Why am I doing this? Do want to I impress others or impact them? Do I want to be seen or felt?" Dig deep to understand your motives every step of the way.

CUP OF
TEA

"If you set out to be liked, you would be prepared to compromise on anything at any time, and you would achieve nothing."

—Margaret Thatcher

L ET'S FACE IT: no matter what you do in life, some people won't like you. That's okay. No matter what you do, there's going to be a time and a place when people are going to have an issue with you, and it won't necessarily be about what you're doing. They may appreciate it or even love it, but the very fact that you're the person doing what you're doing may upset them. But don't change who you are to accommodate people and make them like you! You can't possibly know why they don't like you—maybe it's because of their past experiences or past relationships, or maybe you just look like an individual who did something wrong to them. Don't take it personally! You're not going to be everyone's cup of tea.

Understand who you are and appreciate who you are. Once you focus on your natural God-given abilities, everything will fall in line no matter who likes (or doesn't like) what you're doing. What you think about yourself and what your motives are is what genuinely matters. If you let negative information or negative individuals cloud your judgment about what you're doing or why you're doing it, you will never reach your goal.

Someone once told a good friend of mine a bold-faced lie about my character, and to this day, I still don't truly know why seeing as I had never had a negative encounter or poor relationship with that person. I'm glad that my friend told me what was said, because I now know how they feel and I can keep my distance from them. Apparently, that individual thought that telling my friend something false about me would change my friend's perspective of me, but that kind of negative talk doesn't work—it just reinforces the fact that people are not going to like you. If your intentions are pure, though, you don't have time to ask why. Again, stay positive and stay who you are. I read somewhere that "everyone's moral compass isn't pointed in the same direction." There will be people who will never understand your motives or passion because they haven't walked in your shoes.

Where you're from and how you look may influence someone's perspective of you before you even get a chance to show them what you have to offer, but when you reach an opportunity, show up and show out! As my mentor DJ Jess says, "Always be prepared—you never know when someone will give you the opportunity to shine!" Everything that makes you unique can be a game-changer. Sip on that!

THE WRAP-UP

WE ALL HAVE a light within us, and it's up to you to regulate how bright you'll be. No matter what, though, be yourself at all times! Trying to be someone you aren't is the most selfish thing you could do to yourself. The light that's within you is unique and deserves the opportunity to shine.

If you are doing things that are in line with who you naturally are, you'll effortlessly attract people and opportunities to yourself. You *will* be the right one for the job; you *will* be the go-to person. Others will see the light within you even if they don't always tell you what they see. Don't worry about telling someone how important or special you are, either. In his book *The Little Red Book of Selling,* Jeffrey Gitomer said, "If you tell someone about you, it's bragging, but if others talk about you, it's proof." And here's the last takeaway: not everyone is going to want, accept, or know how to receive your energy. Make peace with that and keep on moving.

ACCOUNTABILITY SHEET

Your Compass

What do you value and why?

1.

_____

_____

_____

2.

_____

_____

_____

3.

_____

_____

_____

IN THE NEXT 24 HRS, I WILL...

"DON'T
S.O.N. ME!"

"When you talk, you are only repeating what you already know, but when you listen, you may learn something new."

—DALAI LAMA

ONE OF THE best things you can do is be excited for a person who's excited for him- or herself. Why not? Think about the individuals who give suggestions that you don't take and then who don't support you because you're winning without implementing their ideas. That's sad. Some people go to the gym every day, and if they are happy about losing one pound or lifting one more set than they did yesterday, celebrate it! Be happy for them! Let's celebrate each other's greatness. It takes hard work and dedication to do something consistently and get results.

Don't you hate it when you have good news and someone tries to S.O.N. you? I'll break it down for you. First, the S stands for Squash. Have you ever told a friend or a family member some good news, and the first thing they do is point out the negatives? How likely are you to tell that person any more good news? Or *any* news, for that matter? But here's the thing: they may not realize they're being so negative. I want you to be ready if you experience it.

Next, the O part of S.O.N. That's the One-Upper. Everyone knows that one guy or gal who has done it better, sooner, or more times than you. No matter how happy you are, they will find a way to one-up you and bring it back to *their* accomplishments. Who cares about what they have to say? No, actually, listen to them if you can stomach it—they tend to have beneficial information, because a one-upper likes to brag about who and what they know. If you want to see what they are about, ask them to connect you with their point of contact. Put that mouth to work!

Last comes the N, which stands for Non-Important. When someone is nonchalant about your good news, don't overexaggerate the story to get a rise out of them. Just find someone who may appreciate what you have to say. I have to remember this part of S.O.N. when my daughter tells me about giants and how they are real and could squash her. And she doesn't mean the 6-foot-plus people who might seem like a giant to a 7-year-old—we're talking about the 50-foot-tall people who live somewhere near our house.

I celebrate you! I celebrate the fact that you want to move on and think outside the box so you can focus on your dreams. Celebrating each other is an exchange of positive energy, and it's a euphoric feeling. It's okay if a person did something you wouldn't usually do—what matters is that they're happy. Let's be happy for each other even though our roles and our paths to happiness are different. That's okay! The main thing is to value the person and to understand why they are so happy. Be honored that they want to share with you in the first place.

THE WRAP-UP

ONE OF THE worst feelings in the world is wanting to share good news with a loved one or someone you look up to only to be disregarded. Have you ever felt that way? I'm not the only one, right? Good! Don't do that to others! If someone is sharing news with you and if you have time to talk, genially ask more questions about the situation. Be happy *they* are happy and willing to share their good news with you. And remember to say "Thank you for sharing!" That will create a welcoming environment for more conversations. Some news may not be considered "good news," but you will have set the tone for that person to feel comfortable talking to you.

ACCOUNTABILITY SHEET

Correct responses to S.O.N. (aka how to be the opposite)

SQUASH

> Genuinely express enthusiasm towards someone's good news even if it doesn't involve you.

ONE-UPPER

> Listen to someone's good news without interjecting your own story unless they ask if you have experienced the same thing.

NON-IMPORTANT

> Ask questions to keep the person talking about their good news. Help them savor the moment.

Bonus: The Prize

This section is totally off-script for a reason. There's an old saying that goes, "If you want to hide something from someone, put it in a book." That's the goal of this section: I hope you take something from this book and pass it along, but with an added gift. In this box, you can write a message and add a check, a handwritten letter, or cash to give to someone you want to invest in. This gift can be words of wisdom or a small love offering they can invest in their dreams. Good luck!

IN THE NEXT 24 HRS, I WILL...

CURVEBALLS!

"Surround yourself with people who reflect who you want to be and how you want to feel. Energies are contagious."

—Rachel Wolchin

LIFE IS GOING to throw you all kinds of curveballs. That's inevitable. Some things you can avoid, but some things you won't be able to avoid...and that's where the growth process comes into play, because when life happens, you have to show up! I believe people have a way of throwing curveballs at you every day. We have to see them coming—if we don't, they'll attach themselves to us. Consider the law of energy. It says that energy can neither be created nor destroyed; rather, it can only be transformed or transferred from one form to another. Sometimes people when have their own life experiences and adversities going on, they throw them at you. I call that a transferred-energy ball.

Here's the good news: you don't have to catch every energy ball that's thrown at you. I occasionally do have to laugh to myself when I see individuals with a scar near their eyes. In my mind, I think, "What?? You didn't see that one coming?" Maybe that's petty of me to say that. But it's true! We've all come into contact with people with bad juju. What do you do when you come across that? Combat the negative energy with positive energy, that's what. When someone has negative energy they want you to have—they might even try to throw it into your lap—avoid that ball of mess! It's not yours to carry, nor is it yours to keep. You'll have plenty of issues and situations of your own to deal with.

Isn't it lovely to be around someone who's peaceful and pleasant? Now think of the opposite: the person who has an issue with everything and everyone. If you aren't careful, they can pull you right into their miserable world. I encourage you not to take their negativity personally. You never know what others are going through or how they're dealing with it. The only thing you *can* control is what energy you let into your own life.

I once knew someone who was so negative that every time they would call me, I had to take a deep breath because I knew what the conversation was going to be like. Finally, one day I made a promise to myself that no matter what they said, I would change the negative narrative into a positive one. When I did, at first they didn't know how to take it. I guess they were mostly talking to themselves at that point, and to a degree, they were, because I refused to invest any of my time and energy into their negativity. Eventually, they caught on, and our conversations were much better. Shorter, too. Choose to be happy! If someone is constantly upsetting you because of their bad vibes or conversation, stop catching the ball they're tossing to you. Let them play with someone else!

THE WRAP-UP

YOU ARE NOT responsible for someone else's happiness. However, you *are* responsible for your own. Like I've said before, the standard you create for yourself will be the standard that people will associate with you. Negative vibes and conversations are draining. The only good that comes from them is that afterwards, you'll be more aware of who to communicate with. You owe it to yourself to be surrounded by love and light! The more you see and hear, the more you can give. Both positive and negative vibes are contagious—it's up to you which ones you surround yourself with.

NOT EVERY
DOOR

"Just because the door is open, it doesn't mean you should walk through it."

—SETH MILLER

"The inability to delegate is one of the biggest problems I see with managers at all levels."

—ELI BROAD

If someone in your family or workplace comes to you and says, "You're great at X—could you do that for me, please?" what do you say? Let me guess—it all depends on who's asking, right? Wrong! How do you know when to say no? How do you know if something is worth your time? First, let's hit on time, real smooth. You might not like what I'm about to say, but understand that I'm here to help you, not to make you feel all warm inside. Ready? Here it is: there's no such thing as "time management." That felt good to type! It's true, though. How can you manage *time* itself? You can't, that's how!

What you *can* do is manage yourself and make sure that you perform certain tasks within certain time slots. You have to decide every day what you'll do in your next 24 hours. If I could have 25 hours in the day, I would use the extra one to catch up on sleep! Ha! You thought I would say something profound about that extra hour, right? Nope! Real me equals real talk! I have to get the best sleep within my ideal amount of sleeping time. Eight full hours would have me feeling low and sluggish all day—for me, five to six hours is optimal. That gives me enough non-sleeping time to accomplish the things I have to do as well as the things I want to do.

Who's asking for the favor shouldn't matter—what should matter is your intent. Are you the only one who can do the job? If so, why? Do you like the power of people coming to you and you only? Get my drift? That is not the way of a black-collar hustler, or a good leader for that matter. Ask yourself, "Is this urgent? Can I delegate? Do I have time to put value into this task?" Let's look at an example.

When someone puts you in a position to grow, you won't forget it. I know I won't. The person who did that for me was a guy named Rick. He was in charge of a specific area in a well-known organization. Many tasks came along with the job, and Rick knew that he couldn't do everything on his own. That's where I came into the picture. Rick saw something in me that I didn't see—he challenged me to think about and see things as a leader, not just a member. He cultivated the leader inside of me without me even knowing it. Pretty soon, Rick was able to get other things accomplished because he had taught me how to do what he did, which meant that we had two subject matter experts. Some people might have thought that Rick had manipulated me to do his work for him, but that wasn't the case, not by far. He was able to look at his tasks and sort out when and what he could teach me. Some things only he had access to, while other things he could quickly go over with me and then let me handle it with little or no supervision. Rick knew what kind of person it took to do the job right, and he trusted me to do it right. He showed me that not every open door was meant for him to walk through—sometimes, that door was there to open more doors for others.

THE WRAP-UP

THE ABILITY TO create opportunities for others or delegate tasks so that others can grow is arguably one of the greatest attributes of being a leader. It's amazing how much time you can give back to yourself when you share your knowledge with a young Jedi. (Look it up!) There's a huge difference between *telling* someone what to do and *showing* them how to do it. You would appreciate it a lot more, too, if someone showed you the ropes and then let you walk in your own greatness.

However, not everyone is willing to share their experiences with you so that you can succeed. If that is the case, watch them closely, because successful people display habits that can be easily copied *if* you are willing to do so. Establishing those habits may require you to wake up every morning at 4:15, for example. Who knows? No matter the situation, when you are tasked to do something, make sure you manage yourself and prioritize your tasks within the time they need to be done.

ACCOUNTABILITY SHEET

Is the task urgent? Could you delegate it to someone else? Do you have time to put value into the task?

	Urgent	*Not Urgent*
Important	Do it now	Plan it
Not Important	Delegate it	Drop it

IN THE NEXT 24 HRS, I WILL...

PLASTIC
PLANT

"Sometimes exhaustion is not a result of too much time spent on something, but of knowing that in its place, no time is spent on something else."

—JOYCE RACHELLE

I ONCE FOUND my daughter playing around in my man cave. My first thought was "Keep out!" It's a place for men—manly things are everywhere, like sports memorabilia ("Go, Lions!" for my Detroit readers), cigars, alcohol, and other things that loudly proclaim "Man cave!" However, when you have a princess in a house, everything is her domain.

My daughter wanted to water a plant that was in the corner. Keep in mind that my man cave is in a basement. The only type of plant I could think of that would look nice but also be low-maintenance was a beautiful plastic plant. At the age of four, however, my daughter felt that all plants needed water.

I had to stop her. "What are you doing, Fat-Fat?" I asked. (Yes, that's the name I gave her due to her chubby cheeks.) Sure, at her age, she was right for thinking that way...but at my age, watering a plastic plant sounded like the craziest thing possible to do.

I'm sure you agree—why *would* you water a plastic plant? But guess what? We do it all the time without even noticing it. We pour our time and energy into things and people that are not beneficial to us and that don't help us grow. That's not to say things and people aren't worth your time, of course. Just make sure you know the value of pouring out your knowledge and time.

Yes, we've all watered those plastic plants at some point in time. The question is, why would you continue to do so? Think of a person in a difficult situation who asks you for advice or input. You hate to see them in that situation, and you feel obligated to pour sound advice into them. But then how do you feel when they've sat and listened to you and then still keep doing the same thing that got them into trouble to begin with? Some people just want to vent—they have no intention of changing their situation. That's where the phrase "Misery loves company" comes from. Others love to hear the sound of their own voice and desire to waddle on in their situation (which nine times out of ten they put themselves into) and refuse to get themselves out of it.

Are you watering a plastic plant? What do you think is going to come from that? Sounds funny when you read it out loud, huh? Ultimately, a person's situation will only change when they choose to take action. We've all fallen victim to misery-loving people who keep wanting more and more water even though they won't make use of it. There will come a day when you'll ask yourself, "Is this worth my time?"

Remember, time is different than money. We waste money all the time on frivolous things, and that's natural. We can make that money back if we're smart. What we can't get back, though, is time. Time is the most valuable resource known to man. How many plastic plants are you watering?

THE WRAP-UP

WHEN YOU UNDERSTAND the value of your time and the resources and wealth that time gives us, you'll not only be running away from the crowd, you will be running away from distractions. When you start to analyze the time and energy you put into things that don't matter, sooner or later you will get tired of wasting your hard-earned time on something that isn't making your life or someone else's life better.

ACCOUNTABILITY SHEET

List 3 things you do every day that are value-added.

_____

_____

_____

List 3 people in your life who are helping you grow and why.

_____

_____

_____

IN THE NEXT 24 HRS, I WILL...

NEVER
STOP

"Do what's right no matter who's looking."

—Seth Miller

"Don't live the same day over and over again and call that a life. Life is about evolving mentally, spiritually, and emotionally."

—Germany Kent

Why do you do what you do? It might sound silly, but it's a fair question to ask yourself. You wake up to go to school or you work to pay bills, but why? Are you doing what you are doing to become a better you, or are you doing it to be better than others? I once knew a lady I'll call Mary. She made it her business to be the first person at work and also the last to leave. No one could take away the fact that she was a hard worker. She would boast about what she did and what she was in charge of and she would point out who wasn't doing their job correctly. She took pride in telling people what to do even if it was outside of her lane. (Do you know any Marys?)

One day, I stopped her in the hallway and said, "I see you getting it on over there and always working! Are you trying to put kids through college?"

She laughed and said, "Heck, no, I don't have kids! I want to outwork these lazy people, especially Tim!"

"What's wrong with Tim?" I asked.

"He's never around when I need him, and he leaves before the boss does," she explained.

"Oh, that's crazy!" I said, and walked away. What she didn't know is that I knew Tim very well. He was the hardest-working person in that department. The reason why Tim seemed to never be around was because he was taking care of things his boss asked him to take care of, and he would leave before the boss did because he produced quality work day in and day out. Do you know a Tim or a Mary? Are *you* a Tim or Mary?

Again, I ask you, why do you do what you do? Are you doing things for the right reasons, or are you trying to impress someone? Please take a second and think about what you are tasked to do every day and how much effort you put into it. The fact is, giving your 100% *is* always good enough...and it's also a fact that even when you do give 100%, people will still have a problem with what you do and how you do it. (See the "Cup of Tea" chapter for more about this.) Everyone's grind and motivations are different.

Just keep your own reasons in the forefront of your mind every time you do something. They're the intangible things that guide your purpose: your background, your beliefs, your family, your fears, maybe even a desire to break the cycle of generational thought processes.

THE WRAP-UP

I'M THE FIRST man in my family to receive a higher-learning degree, and I'm very proud of that. I'm most proud of the fact that my children will understand that this is now the standard for them. They will realize that nothing will ever be handed to them without working for it and that they will receive everything they put out. I tell them to enjoy a 70% prize when they put in a 70% effort. Yes, 70% is considered passing, but it's substandard to me.

Dig this: your competition isn't other people or your family members, your competition is your procrastination, your ego, the unhealthy food you're eating, and the books you neglect. The negative behavior you're nurturing and your lack of creativity are your competitors to success—they're what stand in your way. Some people may think my standards for myself are too extreme, but so what? What are your standards?

ACCOUNTABILITY SHEET

What's Your Motivation?

How do you know you are giving 100%?

_____

_____

_____

What /who motivates you to go hard every day?

_____

_____

_____

IN THE NEXT 24 HRS, I WILL...

YOU ARE
DOPE

"I'm going to show you how great I am!"

—Muhammad Ali

E VERY DAY, WE see images everywhere reminding us how different we are or how we don't measure up to society's standards. Sometimes the person closest to you says, "I remember when you were a little fat little kid in elementary school" even though they now see you as a fit and successful adult! Keep a lookout for the people in your life who constantly find a way to remind you of your past. I encourage you not to take offense when you hear those words—instead, just reflect on how far you've come and say, "Yeah, you're right! Humble beginnings." You have to remember how dope you were and are in order to overcome obstacles.

Constantly hearing about ourselves from others can be a big obstacle in our path to personal growth. Too often, we rely on others for confirmation about what we already know about ourselves. We have to purposefully position things in our daily route through life to remind us of who we truly are. Try to have words of affirmation around your home to remind you of how dope you are. The notes might say "Smile anyway!" or "This too shall pass" or "Unbreakable." Those small statements may remind you of situations you've overcome in the past or emotional barriers you've broken through, or they may be positive affirmations you can use to respond to negative situations.

Are you repeating something untrue that someone said about you? Beware! There's power in that, and not the dope kind. You are telling your own mind what you may or may not deserve and putting up mental barriers that will tell you what you are *not* capable of. Give yourself the approval to believe in yourself! Allow yourself to be great! Don't wait for affirmation or approval from others—if you do, you'll be waiting until the cows come home. People may say you aren't really as dope as you think you are, but I'm here to tell you that yes, you *are* dope enough!

THE WRAP-UP

SCIENCE HAS SHOWN the effect of positive and negative words spoken to houseplants. I'm not comparing you to a plant by any means, but what I am trying to get you to understand is that the words we say to and about ourselves are important. Don't wait for others to fill your day with "feel-good juices." That's your job! *You* need to tell yourself how awesome you are! If you need reminders, take a minute and think of all of the things you've gone through over the years. Some of us are lucky to still be alive! If it's too hard for you to remember what you've overcome and how many times you've succeeded, place sticky notes around your home with positive affirmations written on them. Visualize your end results, concentrate your energy, and line up the things now that will add up to the future you want.

ACCOUNTABILITY SHEET

Instructions: Cut these affirmations out and post them where you can see them.

Words of Affirmation

I AM DOPE

SMILE ANYWAY

UNBREAKABLE

YOU GOT THIS

IN THE NEXT 24 HRS, I WILL...

BUILDING YOUR
SQUAD

"Not everyone in your boat is rowing."

—SETH MILLER

"Trust is hard to come by. That's why my circle is small and tight. I'm kind of funny about making new friends."

—EMINEM

Not everybody in your boat is rowing. You have to make sure you analyze the individuals who are in your circle and why they're there. Just because someone is not rowing as hard as you, though, does not mean that they're not useful. We all bring a specific set of skills to the table, and if someone is willing to enhance your team with their gifts, let them. You might have a navigator on your crew, that person who can see things when you can't. They can communicate possible pitfalls to you so that you can make it to your destination more smoothly or maybe even sooner. Your navigator could be a mentor or a spiritual guide. Respect the people in your boat who have traveled through the same waters you're traveling now, because they bring loads of knowledge and information with them.

You may have cheerleaders in your boat as well. They're the ones who keep you moving and motivated. They can tell when you aren't giving 100%, and they hold you accountable. I had a friend who could feel when I wasn't on my square. Weird, right? He would call me and check to see where my headspace was at. You should have someone like that in your corner. Some cheerleaders might get on your nerves when they keep motivating you even when you're not feeling motivated, but they have your best interests at heart—they want you to succeed. Know who they are and take care of them, because they will take care of you.

Be aware of the individuals in your boat who might be quietly drilling holes in the floor of your boat. These are the people we keep around just because they've known us since we were in grade school, or they might be family members. Not everyone in your boat will want to see you make it to shore. That's a sad truth, but still, it's a truth.

Stay focused on your destination and the people who truly want to help you get there! Take a hard look at and analyze the people in your boat. The boat is your life and your dreams, and you want to make sure you have a good crew of individuals who can help you get to where you want to go. You want individuals who *understand* where you want to go.

On the flip side, realize when you are in someone else's boat. Are you rowing or are you quietly drilling holes in their boat? Do you see pitfalls coming that a friend or family member could avoid? Find a way to communicate that information to them OUT OF LOVE, not because you're trying to be right. Do not be that individual! Some of your words may fall on deaf ears. That's okay. Not everyone will be ready to receive what you have to give them, so please be okay with that. There's no reason for you to repeat your thoughts to others and say how ignorant they are for not listening to you. The people you are meant to inspire will come into your life just like you will come into theirs.

If you're in someone else's boat and you find yourself not able to hold yourself to the standards that you set for others in your *own* boat, remove yourself from that other person's boat. Remove yourself to allow someone else to be productive and active in that person's life. Admit to yourself when someone else is heading in a direction that isn't the same as yours.

There's an old saying that goes, "People come into your life for a reason, season, or a lifetime." I believe that's a true statement and that those three scenarios can be simultaneous. The reasons behind people coming into your life may not be clear at the moment, but if you pay attention, there are lessons behind every reason, lessons you may receive later. A season represents a time in your life when you are expanding your thought processes or your network begins to change significantly; a lifetime represents the sum of your reasons and seasons. In other words, there's a reason why someone comes into your life and helps you move to a different stage that could improve or change your path for your entire lifetime. We are all connected to each other in some way, but it's up to each of us to see how those connections happen in our lives. Sails up and bon voyage!

THE WRAP-UP

SOMETIMES THE PEOPLE around you won't understand your journey or your grind. They don't need to—if it's not for them, you can find other people to have in your boat. True friendship is undeniably imperative for your mental and emotional well-being. With a solid support network in place, you can meet just about any challenge life throws at you. Plus, you can enjoy everything so much more when you're surrounded by companions who appreciate you and truly "get" you. But what's the definition of a true friend? What makes for a good friendship, and how can you tell if you're cultivating one?

ACCOUNTABILITY SHEET

Name 4 people who are genuinely in your boat:

_____
_____
_____
_____

How are they contributing to your journey?

_____
_____
_____
_____
_____
_____
_____
_____
_____
_____

Name someone who's in your boat but shouldn't be:

_____
_____
_____

IN THE NEXT 24 HRS, I WILL...

THE ART OF
MACARONI AND
CHEESE

*"Those that dare not to dream big are cowards, for
they fear to expose the already great potentials
embedded inside of them."*

—AULIQ-ICE

ANYONE WHO KNOWS me knows that I love macaroni
and cheese. Not just any mac and cheese, but the kind
that's oven-baked with five or six different cheeses in it. That's
the key to an excellent macaroni and cheese! It makes me feel
good when it's made right. The taste reminds me of my childhood and the family get-togethers we had back in the day.
Word to the wise: not all mac and cheeses are created equal.
You have to have at least twenty years of experience and three
good references before I taste yours! Mac and cheese might
not be that serious for you, but it is for me. It's a love of mine!

I want you to think about what you love. Why do you love
it? What do you love about it? Are you feeling happy yet?
Good! Keep that feeling close when people ask you why you
love what or whom you love. Keep that feeling when people
try to judge you for believing in something that you can see

clear as day even when they can't. Here are a few things to be mindful of:

1. DON'T BE JUDGMENTAL. There may come a time when someone you care about doesn't understand your vision and your passion. That's okay—it's your vision, not theirs. Even when people share the same passion as you, they may provide you with a different perspective. Don't build a wall so high that no one can come over it and you can't see past it. Ideas are meant to evolve, just like we are. Often, ideas may come from someone you feel doesn't have much credibility or experience. People will surprise you with the wisdom they have collected throughout their lives. We all come from different walks of life, and we all have valuable information to provide. Not everyone will seem successful, but they may have years of experience of what *not* to do.

2. YOU DON'T KNOW IT ALL. If someone is respecting you and your passion, be willing to listen to them. They may have experienced the same barrier that you are currently facing, and they may have overcome it. Sometimes we get so complacent and stuck in our ways that we think people outside of the group don't have anything to bring to the table, but we have two ears and one mouth for a reason: to listen twice as much as we speak. Practice holding your thoughts to yourself! You might learn something new. And even if you think you've learned everything there is to learn about a specific subject, keep learning anyway. I

guarantee there's more to it than you think! Keep a growth mindset in life and be a student of learning. A growth mindset versus a fixed mindset can differentiate people in a huge way. For example, when it comes to having skills, someone with a fixed mindset will think those skills are something you're born with, while the person with a growth mindset probably thinks skills come from hard work and can always be improved. Likewise, someone with a fixed mindset tends to blame others and get discouraged when it comes to setbacks, while a person with a growth mindset will use setbacks as a wake-up call to work harder the next time. Once you change the way you perceive everyday obstacles and challenges, the way you receive information from others will change as well.

3. ACKNOWLEDGE GOOD POINTS MADE BY OTHER PEOPLE. Let's get back to mac and cheese for a minute. The best thing about it is that there are hundreds of ways to make it. Since I'm a self-proclaimed connoisseur of the dish, I would love to learn something new to boost my skills. What if a skilled hamburger-maker suggested that I make mac and cheese with Thousand Island dressing in it? Sounds crazy, right? However, he's a pro in his lane, and he might be on to something. It might actually taste good! Many businesses go under because they are afraid to try something different and see how it will go, but trying different things can only make you more experienced and better at whatever you're trying to do. Again,

beware of your wall of knowledge. We can always learn more and in turn love more. If you can visualize something, then it's most definitely possible! It's up to you to take the first step forward. I'm telling you, if you are reading this, you'll have more chances to connect with someone and make a difference in your life and theirs.

THE WRAP-UP

DON'T BE so judgmental. There was a time you didn't know anything! Now's the time to tell people what you've learned *and* to listen to others. Just because you learned something new doesn't mean you know everything there is to know about that subject. Be a teacher and a forever student. If someone has a good point or is willing to help you improve your current situation, leave your pride and your ego at the door and see how far you can go without that extra baggage.

CONCLUSION

THERE YOU HAVE it: all the answers to the world! I'm just kidding, of course. I'm blessed to have had positive and negative influences in my life; luckily, the positive ones made good impressions and bad ones didn't kill me!

If you apply the tools that are within these pages, you will become a better person and enjoy a better life. And remember, take the time to be happy. When you are happy, everyone wants to hang around you!

Thank you for taking the time to read and use this book. I hope you learned something new or maybe confirmed what you already knew. You don't have to be broken to become better! Thank you for your support and love. Now, buy another book for a friend or mentee since you've written all over this one, right? Share the knowledge and water your seed.

SETH THE SPEAKER

ABOUT
THE AUTHOR

S ETH A. MILLER is a 20 year Air Force veteran
stationed at Scott AFB, Illinois. He is 39 years old.
Seth Miller was born in Detroit, Michigan, on 10 April
1980. He attended the Benjamin Oliver Davis Aerospace
Technical High School in Detroit. He was a member of the
school AFJROTC Junior Reserve Officer Training Corp pro-
gram. After graduating from high school, Seth enlisted in the
Air Force in 1998 and arrived at Lackland AFB, Texas, in
December of that year for basic training. Upon graduating
HVAC Technical School at Sheppard AFB, Texas he has
been assigned to Whiteman AFB, McChord AFB, Osan AB
Korea, Anderson AFB Guam, and Scott AFB. He was also
deployed to Bright Star, Egypt, Ali Al Salem, Al Udeid,
Balad, and Mazar-i-Sharif. He has completed a Bachelor of
Arts degrees in Human Resources and Business Development
at Park University. Seth is also, the Area 6 Director of Toast-
masters in the Illinois and Greater St. Louis district.

He's and award-winning speaker and John Maxwell
certified trainer and coach. Seth signature talks are:
Leadership, Resiliency, Diversity and Power of influence.

CONTACT

To order additional copies of this book, contact the author:

SETH MILLER
Paradigm Shift Consulting
Email: smiller48205@gmail.com
Website: www.seththespeaker.com

REFERENCES

Poem from Rudyard Kipling: IF *A Choice of Kipling's Verse by* (1943)

Quote from Darth Vader: *Star Wars* (1977)

Quote from Anna Freud: *Quotations for All Occasions* by Mira Balachandran (2009)

Quote from Swami Vivekananda: *Words to Live By* by Eknath Easwaran (2010)

Quote from Maya Angelou: *Phenomenal Woman: Four Poems Celebrating Woman* by Maya Angelou (2011)

Quote from Tony Gaskins: *Single is Not a Curse* by Tony Gaskins (2013)

Quote from Tony Robbins: *Awaken the Giant Within* by Tony Robbins (2007)

Quote from Paul Bear Bryant: *Don't Play for the Tie: Bear Bryant on Life* by Paul Bear Bryant (2006)

Quote from Kresley Cole: *Dark Skye* by Kresley Cole (2014)

Quote from Robert W. Service: *The Big Detour* by C. Wayne Owens (2005)

Quote from Margaret Thatcher: *Shut Up and Say Something* by Karen Friedman (2010)

Quote from Dalai Lama: *Nothing is Impossible: Build a New Life in Seven Stages* by Geraldine Appel (2016)

Quote from Rachel Wolchin: *Imagine Your Success Path, Believe in the Impossible* by Joyce Mbaya (2011)

Quote from Eli Broad: *The Art of Being Unreasonable: Lessons in Unconventional Thinking* by Eli Broad (2012)

Quote from Germany Kent: *The Rewired Life* by Erica Spiegelman (2018)

Quote from Muhammad Ali: *I Am the Greatest* by John Micklos Jr. (2004)

Quote from Eminem: *Meaning of Life* by Ryan D'Agostino (2009)

Made in the USA
Coppell, TX
20 March 2021